Roo's Rocket

Written by M J Hooton

Illustrated by Kayla Stark

Collins

I'm Roo. I leap and bound around — like a kangaroo!

3

"So boring," I complain to Craig.

"Come on Roo, don't distract Craig," Miss Hassan says. "You might enjoy this!"

"We need a spectacular planet display for the reading corner," Miss Hassan explains.

"How might we travel to a planet?"

"In a rocket!" I shout out.

"Rockets zoom higher than the skies and rescue us from the beasts out there!"

"Sounds cool." Miss Hassan grins.
I feel proud.

Yes, Miss, it's *mega* cool, I think, starting my rocket.

I turn a cream pot into a firm support for my rocket. I paint it blue, like my uniform.

I glue on a point, then smooth it with clay.

Finished!

My rocket flies into blue skies.
Soon darkness surrounds it.

There's no sound apart from my rocket
zipping by all the planets I can think of.

First, red Mars, then Saturn's rings
At Jupiter, there's a problem.

vroom!

I hear the beasts on Jupiter, chirping and clicking. I freak out.

Go rocket, deploy goo shooters!

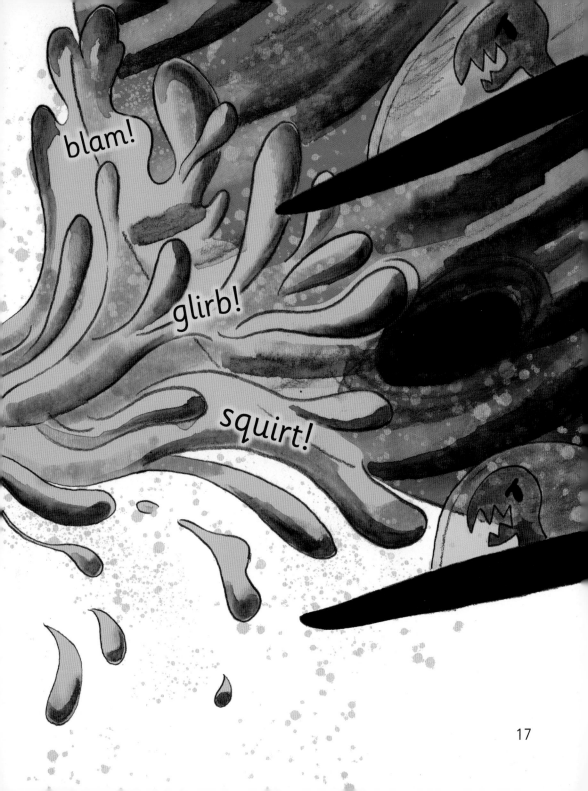

"What a mess!" Miss Hassan says. "Is that a planet Roo?"

My lip is wobbling. I didn't mean to
squirt the paint.

"I didn't model a planet," I explain. "I was too into my rocket."

"This rocket is outstanding. There's room on the planet display for a rocket, too," Miss Hassan says. "But first, let's clean this mess."
That turns my frown around.

Roo's feelings

 Review: After reading

Use your assessment from hearing the children read to choose any GPCs, words or tricky words that need additional practice.

Read 1: Decoding

- Reread page 19. Ask: What does it mean when someone's lip is **wobbling**? (e.g. *it's trembling*) Does it show how they are feeling? (e.g. *they are on the verge of tears*)
- Remind the children to break down longer words into chunks as they read. Tell them to check that they sound out words containing "u" and "ue" correctly – as /u/, /oo/ or /yoo/.

  spec-tac-u-lar   res-cue   u-ni-form   glue   supp-ort

- Challenge the children to take turns to read a sentence aloud. Ask: Can you blend in your head when you read each word?

Read 2: Prosody

- Let the children work in pairs to practise a dramatic reading of pages 16 and 17.
- Ask them to think about how they will read Roo's story and which lines they would give extra emphasis to.
- Encourage the children to practise saying the sound words in different ways. How might a **blam** sound different to a **squirt**?

Read 3: Comprehension

- Say sometimes people can lose focus or get too involved with what they're doing and don't notice that they might be making a mess or causing some bother. Can you think of any examples in the book where this happened to Roo?
- Turn to pages 22 and 23. Challenge the children to find an action or event that links with each emotion. Ask questions such as:
  - Why was Roo bored?
  - Who made Roo feel proud?
  - Why do you think Roo got worried after their "freak out"? Encourage children to look back at the story if they're unsure.

To find out more about this book and the author go to: collins.co.uk/BooksLikeMe